This book belongs to

_____

_____

Illustrations by Pamela Garcia

Thank you for choosing *Little Cutie Fairies, Volume Three – Forest Fairies.*

Coloring pictures is an enjoyable and accessible activity that offers a range of benefits for individuals of all ages and skill levels. Whether you are seeking stress relief, a creative outlet, or a moment of mindfulness, this practice can help you find balance and tranquility in your daily life. Witnessing the transformation of a blank page into a vibrant work of art can boost your self-confidence and self-esteem. It provides a tangible result that you can be proud of, regardless of your artistic background

There is no right or wrong way to color a picture. Use your imagination. Try a variety of tools – colored pencils, markers, pens, pastels, and crayons. If you use markers or pens, place a piece of cardboard or heavy paper so your coloring does not bleed onto the next page. The pictures appear only on one side of the paper to help with bleeding. It also allows you to remove a page for framing, if you wish. There is a page where you can experiment with mixing colors.

The fact that you have chosen to support my work warms my heart. I hope this book brings you as many hours of joy as designing it did for me. Know that these pictures were a labor of love. I am thrilled to know they have found a good home with you.

Grab a cup of coffee or tea, sit down, relax, and have fun.
You deserve some quiet time.

Thank you again for your support.

COLOR SAMPLER

Not sure what color to use? Try it here or try mixing colors together.

Congratulations. You've finished coloring all those cute fairies. I hope you had fun. If you enjoyed the experience, please leave me a review on Amazon.

To view more of my coloring books, please visit www.prgarcia1.com. Sign up for my newsletter and receive free coloring , coloring tips, and notification of new releases.

I appreciate your support. Never forget to have a little fun every day. Spred goodwill throughout your world. And remember to keep an eye out for fairies. You'll never know where they're hiding.

An Adult Coloring Book

Little Fairy Cuties

volume One

An Adult Coloring Book

Little Fairy Cuties

volume Two

www.prgarcias1.com

PRGARCIA1